W9-CIM-600

WHO WAS SITTING BULL?

And Other Questions about the Battle of Little Bighorn

Judith Pinkerton Josephson

LERNER PUBLICATIONS COMPANY · MINNEAPOLIS

A Word about Language

English word usage, spelling, grammar, and punctuation have changed over the centuries. We have preserved original spellings and word usage in the quotations included in this book.

Thanks to Mickey and John Lester for access to their extensive Little Bighorn collection and to Edith, Karen, my critique group, and editor Ann Kerns for asking the right questions

Lerner Publications Company
A division of Lerner Publishing Group, Inc.
241 First Avenue North
Minneapolis, MN 55401 U.S.A.

Website address: www.lernerbooks.com

Library of Congress Cataloging-in-Publication Data

Josephson, Judith Pinkerton.
    Who was Sitting Bull? : and other questions about the Battle of Little Bighorn / by Judith Pinkerton Josephson.
        p.   cm. — (Six questions of American history)
    Includes bibliographical references and index.
    ISBN 978-0-7613-5230-3 (lib. bdg. : alk. paper)
    1. Little Bighorn, Battle of the, Mont., 1876—Juvenile literature. I. Title.
E83.876.J67 2011
978.004'9752—dc22   2010033372

Manufactured in the United States of America
1 – DP – 12/31/10

TABLE OF CONTENTS 4

THE SIX
QUESTIONS
HELP YOU
DISCOVER THE
FACTS!

INTRODUCTION

In the mid-1800s, the western United States had tens of thousands of miles of open land. There were few roads or large cities. Pioneers streamed west to build farms or ranches on this open land. Wealthy Americans built railroads and dug coal mines. But the West was already home to many people—the Native Americans.

Native Americans resented people settling on land where they had lived for centuries. The West's new settlers thought of Indians as obstacles to frontier life. "The American people need the country the Indians now occupy," read a South Dakota newspaper article. This clash over land and different ways of life led to battles between Native American warriors and U.S. soldiers. To stop the fighting, the U.S. government promised to protect Native Americans' rights. But the government often broke these promises.

In June 1876, several Native American groups gathered in Montana along the Little Bighorn River. Fierce fighting between Indians and U.S. soldiers followed. Warriors surrounded the U.S. military leader, Lieutenant Colonel George Armstrong Custer, and his men. In less than one hour, Custer and all his men lay dead. This famous Battle of Little Bighorn was a disaster for the U.S. military. What Native American tribes were involved?

Amos Bad Heart Bull (1869–1913), a Lakota historian, drew this image of the Battle of Little Bighorn.

4

LITTLE BIGHORN BATTLEFIELD, MONTANA TERRITORY, 1876

■ LITTLE BIGHORN
BATTLEFIELD

IDAHO
TERRITORY

MONTANA
TERRITORY

WYOMING
TERRITORY

DAKOTA
TERRITORY

MINNESOTA

WISCONSIN

MICHIGAN

VERMONT

MAINE

NEW
HAMPSHIRE

MASSACHUSSETTS

NEW
YORK

UTAH
TERRITORY

NEBRASKA

IOWA

RHODE ISLAND

CONNECTICUT

COLORADO
TERRITORY

ILLINOIS

INDIANA

OHIO

PENNSYLVANIA

NEW JERSEY

DELAWARE

MARYLAND

KANSAS

MISSOURI

WEST
VIRGINIA

VIRGINIA

ARIZONA
TERRITORY

NEUTRAL
STRIP

INDIAN
TERRITORY
(UNORGANIZED)

ARKANSAS

KENTUCKY

NORTH
CAROLINA

NEW MEXICO
TERRITORY

TENNESSEE

SOUTH
CAROLINA

ATLANTIC
OCEAN

MISSISSIPPI

ALABAMA

GEORGIA

TEXAS

LOUISIANA

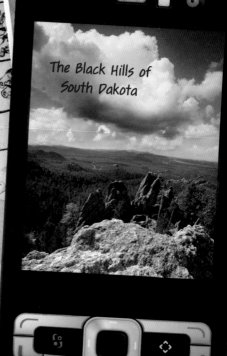

The Black Hills of
South Dakota

Buffalo roam the Black Hills in this modern photo. In the early 1800s, tens of thousands of buffalo roamed the Great Plains.

ONE TROUBLE BREWING

Many Native American tribes once roamed the American West. Of these, the Lakota Sioux and the Cheyenne were two of the largest.

Seven Native American groups—about fifty thousand people—called themselves Lakota. (The Lakota and other related tribes had first been called Sioux by their enemies, the Ojibwe.) All shared similar cultures. In the early 1800s, the Lakota Sioux farmed land along the Mississippi River in modern-day Minnesota and Wisconsin. They traveled on foot and lived in scattered groups.

By trading with other tribes and with early white settlers, the Lakota came to own guns and horses. On horseback the Lakota could cover great distances. They moved west, so hunting parties could follow the buffalo herds that roamed the Great Plains.

Modern-day South Dakota's mountainous Black Hills (*Paha Sapa*) were sacred to some Native Americans. In the Black Hills, the Lakota felt close to *Wakan Tanka*, the Great Spirit. The Sioux believed that the Great Spirit was in the sun, the sky, the wind, and in animals.

When Native American hunters killed a buffalo, they offered prayers to its spirit. They wasted no part of this large animal. One buffalo's meat could feed a whole village. The Lakota used buffalo hides to make tipis and clothing. Bones became tools and weapons. Dried buffalo droppings burned in campfires.

tipis | cone-shaped homes made of tall wooden poles covered in animal skins

Sitting Bull was chief of a Lakota band called the Hunkpapa. He was the most famous Sioux leader. Sitting Bull's Lakota name was Tatanka Iyotanka. It meant "buffalo bull."

band | a group within, or a division of, a tribe

BUFFALO HUNTERS

The transcontinental railroad, completed in 1869, joined America's eastern and western coasts. Americans could travel by train from the Atlantic Ocean to the Pacific Ocean. Trains carried many settlers to the West. They also carried white hunters who shot buffalo only for their hides. Other hunters shot buffalo from train windows, leaving behind mounds of rotting meat and bones. These hunters wasted the Plains Indians most valuable resource, the buffalo.

Sitting Bull was born about 1831 in present-day South Dakota. He grew up to become a warrior, a war chief, and a powerful leader. Sitting Bull was short and stocky, with narrow, piercing eyes and thin lips. People respected and feared him. Sitting Bull wanted a peaceful life, but he did not want to live among white people.

Another large Lakota band was the Oglala. Chief Red Cloud and Crazy Horse were two of their strongest leaders. Crazy Horse's Lakota name was Tasunke Witko. Crazy Horse was born in 1841 in the Black Hills. Called Curly as a boy, he had always been different. He didn't braid his hair, wear fancy clothes, or paint his body. He seldom sang, danced, or took part in ceremonies. Often he stayed away from his people's camp for long periods of time, hunting alone and thinking.

"We want no white men here. The Black Hills belong to me. If the whites try to take them, I will fight."

Sitting Bull

By the age of twelve, Curly longed for a vision to show him his future. For three days, he went without food. He lay on rocks with pebbles between his toes, so he wouldn't sleep. No vision came. Finally, he dreamed about a man on horseback. The man had a painted lightning bolt on his face and hailstones on his body. Behind one ear, he wore a brown pebble. In the dream, a red-backed hawk screamed overhead. When Curly awoke, he vowed to dress for battle just as the man had in his dream.

a dreamlike experience. Some Native American cultures believe that visions give guidance or direction.

Curly's father was named Crazy Horse. When Curly was sixteen, he told his father about the vision. His father said it meant Curly would one day lead his people. Curly's father then gave his son his own name—Crazy Horse. (Many Native Americans had one name at birth and another as adults.)

Artist Robert Lindneux (1871–1970) painted Native American and Old West subjects. In this painting (left), Lindneux imagined what Crazy Horse might have looked like.

Crazy Horse became a warrior and a war chief. He refused to be photographed, so no pictures exist of him. But people who knew him said he had light skin and hair. A long nose divided his narrow face. Like Sitting Bull, Crazy Horse wanted whites out of Indian land.

Another powerful Native American tribe was the Cheyenne. Fearless, fierce, and proud, the Cheyenne had also moved to the Great Plains to hunt buffalo. Cheyenne land stretched from the North Platte River in Colorado all the way to the Rocky Mountains.

Over the years, many Cheyenne had died of diseases such as cholera (caused by germs in food and drinking water) and

Native American hunters chase buffalo in this 1835 painting by George Catlin (1796–1872).

U.S. soldiers surround a Cheyenne village during the Sand Creek Massacre (above). Robert Lindneux painted this depiction in 1936.

smallpox (which passes from person to person). Others died in battles with nearby tribes and with U.S. soldiers. In the 1864 Sand Creek Massacre, U.S. soldiers attacked a Cheyenne village in Colorado. They killed more than 150 people. Most of the victims were women and children.

> the killing of many people at the same time

The Sand Creek Massacre made many Native American warriors angry. They no longer wanted to try to make peace with whites.

NEXT QUESTION

WHAT WAS RED CLOUD'S WAR?

TWO BROKEN PROMISES

By the 1860s, the U.S. government had set aside areas, called reservations, for Native Americans to live in. In return, the government could build roads through these lands and establish forts. The Bozeman Trail to Montana's goldfields cut through the Northern Plains Indians' best hunting grounds.

structures usually protected by high walls, lookout towers, and guarded gates

Between 1866 and 1868, Oglala chief Red Cloud and young warriors from several tribes led attacks against U.S. soldiers and travelers along the Bozeman Trail in Montana and Wyoming territories. These attacks were called Red Cloud's War.

In April 1868, a U.S. government peace commission met with Red Cloud and other Native American leaders at Fort Laramie in Wyoming. The peace commission wanted to end Red Cloud's War. The commission offered the Native Americans a treaty.

The treaty would create the Great Sioux Reservation. The reservation included modern-day South Dakota west of the Missouri River, including the Black Hills. In addition, the treaty said no whites would enter Native American hunting grounds in Wyoming and Montana. Forts along the Bozeman Trail would close. The government would provide food and clothing.

GREAT SIOUX RESERVATION 1868

MONTANA TERRITORY

MISSOURI RIVER

N

DAKOTA TERRITORY

GREAT SIOUX RESERVATION

MINNESOTA

WYOMING TERRITORY

THE BLACK HILLS

CHEYENNE RIVER

THE BADLANDS

WHITE RIVER

JAMES RIVER

MISSOURI RIVER

FORT LARAMIE

NEBRASKA

IOWA

In this 1874 photograph, U.S. Cavalry troops gather wagons and equipment for a scientific and military mission to the Black Hills.

CUSTER AND NATIVE AMERICANS

Custer respected Native Americans for their way of life, their love of the open plains, and their fighting skills. "To me, Indian life . . . is a book of unceasing interest. . . . Some of its pages are frightful. Study him, fight him, civilize him if you can," he wrote. But Custer still considered Native Americans to be savages (wild, violent people). They didn't trust him either. They saw him as part of the government's dishonesty.

In the summer of 1874, Custer led a scientific and military mission to the Black Hills. He brought one thousand men and one hundred wagons. The true purpose of Custer's trip was to search for gold. Miners found flecks of gold in most streams they panned. The Black Hills belonged to the Sioux, but the gold would belong to whites.

LONG HAIR

Most Native Americans never saw Custer in person. But they had heard about the famous cavalry leader. The Lakota and Cheyenne people who had seen Custer began calling him Long Hair because of his flowing blond hair. Others called him Son of the Morning Star.

The Lakota called the tracks left by Custer's wagons a "thieves' trail." They called Custer "chief of thieves." The U.S. government broke other promises made in the Fort Laramie Treaty. It failed to give enough clothing and food to the Native Americans living on the Great Sioux Reservation. People starved and fell ill in cold weather. Native American leaders grew angry. They wanted to take action. On its own, no band of Native Americans was strong enough to stop the intruders. But by working together, several bands might succeed.

NEXT QUESTION

WHERE DID THE INDIANS JOIN FORCES?

Native American women and children stand outside their tipis in this photo from the 1870s. The photo was taken on the Crow Reservation in Montana. Life on a reservation was very hard for most Native Americans.

THREE A GREAT GATHERING

After gold was found in the Black Hills, the news spread quickly. Thousands of people rushed there hoping to become rich. In 1875 the United States tried to buy the Black Hills. The Native Americans refused. "One does not sell the earth upon which the people walk," said Crazy Horse.

The army wanted all Indians who hadn't already done so to settle on reservations by January 31, 1876. Some American citizens didn't think it was right to tell people where to live. But the army's plan won out.

Many Native Americans ignored the order. Federal troops led by General George Crook, General Alfred Terry, and Colonel John Gibbon moved into Indian land to force remaining Native Americans onto reservations. Custer and the 7th Cavalry were part of Terry's command. Battles with the Native Americans over the next year were called the Great Sioux War.

In early June 1876, Sitting Bull invited several tribes to his Rosebud Creek camp in Montana. There he led people in a special ceremony called the Sun Dance. After hours of dancing, forty-five-year-old Sitting Bull had a vision. He saw blue-coated soldiers dying in an Indian village. Like grasshoppers, he said, they fell upside down.

THE SUN DANCE

Many Native Americans practiced the Sun Dance ceremony (left). During this religious ceremony, men cut strips of flesh from their arms. Bleeding and in great pain, they danced, sang, and prayed to the Great Spirit. After hours of this, many dancers had visions.

Sioux warriors charge General George Crook's cavalry soldiers on Rosebud Creek in this 1876 illustration.

THE BATTLE OF THE ROSEBUD

On June 17, 1876, at Rosebud Creek, Crazy Horse and one thousand warriors attacked General Crook's soldiers. In the six-hour battle, Crook's men used up most of their ammunition. Ten U.S. soldiers died, and many were wounded. Crook withdrew his men to Wyoming to wait for help. A week later, they did not take part in the Battle of Little Bighorn.

Sitting Bull's vision inspired thirty-one-year-old Crazy Horse. He led warriors to attack Crook's soldiers at Rosebud Creek. Soon after, Lakota, Cheyenne, and other Indians formed a 3-mile-long (5-kilometer) encampment along the Little Bighorn River in Montana Territory. Here grassy slopes rose to a steep ridge along the river. Indians called this area Greasy Grass.

encampment — a place where a group sets up a camp

Crow Foot, Sitting Bull's son, posed for this portrait in the early 1880s. Crow Foot was only about three years old at the time of the Battle of Little Bighorn.

Seven to twelve thousand men, women, and children set up their tipis. Sitting Bull was overall chief of the great gathering. With him were his two wives, his young son Crow Foot, and an adopted son, One Bull, a warrior.

The Indians knew that nearby soldiers intended to kill them or drive them onto reservations. The Indians planned to fight back, but they also knew the power of the U.S. military. Soldiers carried powerful modern weapons. The Indians also had rifles and pistols. But their strength lay in using spears, knives, war clubs, and bows and arrows.

On the night of June 24, 1876, Sitting Bull climbed to the top of the ridge. As stars shone in the dark sky, he asked the Great Spirit to protect his people. A fight was coming.

NEXT QUESTION

WHEN WOULD THE BATTLE TAKE PLACE?

The Little Bighorn River viewed from a ridge above

FOUR A BAD OMEN

At dawn on June 25, 1876, flocks of birds swooped over the Little Bighorn River. Native Americans who saw them called it a bad omen—a sign that danger lay ahead.

The 7th Cavalry was moving closer to Little Bighorn. Custer's Indian scouts went ahead of the troops to search for signs of Native American warriors. On an overlook, the scouts spotted smoke rising from cooking fires. Edging closer, they saw more than one thousand tipis. Horses and ponies, important in warfare, dotted the hillside. The size of the Native American encampment shocked the scouts. They hurried to tell Custer.

scouts: people used by military groups to gather information

Custer listened to the scouts' report. He looked through field glasses to see for himself. But by that time, a haze of smoke cloaked the encampment. Custer didn't believe his scouts about the camp's size. He called them cowards.

Over the previous two days, Custer had followed the Indians' trail for 70 miles (113 km). After marching all night, his soldiers were tired and hungry. Custer had planned to rest his men and horses and attack at dawn on June 26.

But then soldiers arrived with news. They had found two Sioux youths on a trail.

The Crow scout Ashishishe (also called Curley) poses with his gun across his knee in this 1880s portrait. Ashishishe joined the U.S. Army in 1876 and was part of the scouting party used by the 7th Cavalry at the Battle of Little Bighorn.

The boys had broken into a box of food dropped by the soldiers. Soldiers had killed one boy. But the other escaped and rode off toward the encampment. This news changed Custer's plan of attack. He knew that the surviving boy would sound the alarm. He would tell the Indian leaders where the soldiers were.

Terry, still several miles away in Dakota Territory, had ordered Custer to ride ahead and find the Native American warriors. Then he was to wait for Terry's soldiers to back him up. Instead, Custer decided to attack the encampment immediately.

Custer's Indian scouts thought it foolish for him to attack such a large camp. They felt they would die that day. A Crow scout named Half Yellow Face told Custer, "You and I are both going home today by a road we do not know." Bloody Knife, an Arikara scout, spoke toward the sun. "I shall not see you go down behind the hills tonight," he said.

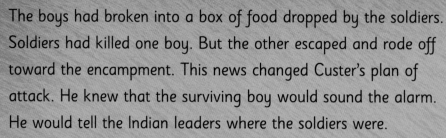

"I have had but little experience in Indian fighting, and Custer has had much, and he is sure he can whip anything he meets."
—General Alfred Terry, June 21, 1876

Alfred Terry

CUSTER'S SOLDIERS

Life for U.S. Cavalry soldiers in the mid-1800s wasn't easy. They had little food and what they had was tasteless. They worked long hours and spent weeks far away from their families. Many of Custer's soldiers had never ridden a horse or shot a rifle before joining the cavalry. Some had recently come to the United States from Europe. They spoke very little English. Other soldiers were poor farm boys. Many believed that joining the cavalry would give them a chance at a new life out west.

By noon the blistering summer heat had soared to 100°F (38°C). Custer rode his horse around the camp barking orders. He wore a blue flannel shirt, buckskin trousers tucked into long boots, and a broad-brimmed army hat. His blond hair was cut short for battle.

buckskin — soft leather made from the hide of a buck, or male deer

Custer split his command into three groups. Captain Frederick Benteen would lead three companies and the pack animals carrying extra ammunition. Benteen would stop the Native Americans from escaping through the valley along the river. Major Marcus Reno and his three companies would charge the village directly. Custer's 210 men would back up Reno and then launch their own attack. Custer had given his orders. The weary soldiers mounted their horses.

companies — units of soldiers

Marcus Reno

Meanwhile, an uneasy mood gripped some in the encampment on June 25. Native American scouts had spotted signs of U.S. soldiers nearby. But children still splashed and swam in the river's clear, cold waters. Boys tended ponies grazing on the hillside. Mothers waved buffalo tail brushes to keep insects away from sleeping babies.

Then the youth who had escaped Custer's soldiers galloped into camp. He reported that nearby troops had killed his companion. "Soldiers coming here!" someone shouted. Horses whinnied. Dogs barked. Mothers gathered their children. Knowing an attack was near, warriors painted their bodies for battle.

In this illustration, U.S. Cavalry troops ride toward the Native American encampment at the beginning of the Battle of Little Bighorn. The image was created by Red Horse, a Lakota chief who was present at the battle.

Crazy Horse (left) and Sitting Bull (center) ride in front of their warriors in this image from the Battle of Little Bighorn.

Women, children, and the elderly fled to hills west of the village. Older men encouraged the younger warriors. Standing in the center of the camp, Sitting Bull shouted to the warriors, "Fear nothing. Go straight in!"

NEXT QUESTION

WHAT HAPPENED DURING THE BATTLE?

Native American warriors chase Major Marcus Reno's cavalry soldiers uphill from the Little Bighorn River. Amos Bad Heart Bull created this illustration in about 1900.

FIVE THE BATTLE BEGINS

Major Reno's soldiers galloped into the southern end of the encampment. As the soldiers charged, hundreds of Lakota and Cheyenne warriors raced forward. Bullets hummed like angry bees. Arrows whirred.

Reno ordered his men to get off their horses. He told them to take cover behind shrubs and cottonwood trees near the river. The exhausted soldiers could barely stand. "Leaves that shake," Sitting Bull said later. "[The soldiers] were brave men, but they were too tired. They swayed to and fro . . . like the limbs of cypresses [trees] in a great wind. Some of them staggered under the weight of their guns."

Without their horses, Reno's soldiers made easy targets. Indians on horseback circled around the soldiers, shooting. In a disorganized retreat, Reno and his men jumped back on their horses and galloped for higher ground. Some scrambled up hillside on foot.

From the river valley, Sitting Bull watched as the Indians attacked the soldiers. Warriors shot, lanced, and kicked soldiers off their horses. As in Sitting Bull's vision, the soldiers fell off their horses upside down. "Our young men rained lead across the river and drove the white braves back," he said.

lanced: stabbed with a weapon called a lance

MILES
0   .25   .50   .75
0   .50   1
KILOMETERS

N

CUSTER
HILL

CUSTER
RIDGE

CALHOUN
HILL

CEMETERY RIDGE

DEEP RAVINE

GREASY GRASS RIDGE

DEEP COULEE

NYE-CARTWRIGHT RIDGE

MEDICINE TAIL COULEE

LUCE RIDGE

INDIAN
ENCAMPMENT

LITTLE
BIGHORN
RIVER

WEIR
POINT

THE
LITTLE BIGHORN
BATTLEFIELD, 1876

Crazy Horse (center, on white horse) leads the charge against Reno's men in this illustration by Bad Heart Bull. Crazy Horse led Lakota and Cheyenne warriors during the battle.

One-third of Reno's 175 soldiers died as they climbed the grassy slopes. A few stayed hidden in the brush. At nightfall they crawled to join the rest on the bluff.

About 3 miles (5 km) from the fighting on the other end of the camp, Crazy Horse rounded up Oglala and more Cheyenne warriors. He painted a lightning bolt on his cheek and hailstones on his body. He tied a pebble behind one ear and sprinkled gopher dust on himself and his horse. Because of his boyhood vision, he believed doing such things would protect him.

"*Ho-ka hey!* It is a good day to fight!" Crazy Horse shouted, as he and his warriors raced toward the fighting. "It is a good day to die! Strong hearts, brave hearts, to the front. Weak hearts and cowards to the rear!" After helping chase Major Reno's soldiers out of the brush, Crazy Horse's warriors moved on to join the fight against Custer.

When Custer got his first up-close view of the encampment teeming with warriors, he realized his scouts had been right. In the distance, he could see Reno and his men battling the Indians—and losing. Custer sent his trumpeter, Giovanni Martini, with a handwritten message for Captain Benteen. It read, "Come on, Big Village, Be quick."

Under attack himself, Custer ordered his men to pull back to a hill. Soldiers fired as they retreated. But many fell wounded or dead along the way. Fighting by Custer's side were his two brothers, Tom and Boston.

Three groups of Indians surrounded Custer and his men. Cheyenne warriors blocked one escape route. The Hunkpapa Sioux, led by war chief Gall, attacked from another side. Crazy Horse and Oglala warriors gathered on a third side.

Custer kept looking for Benteen and his troops. But Benteen had stopped to help Reno and his men. As his men dropped to the ground around him, Custer kept firing. Then he fell. The Son of the Morning Star was dead.

General Custer

Crazy Horse

Three groups of warriors surrounded Custer and his soldiers. This painting by Sioux artist Kills Two (1869–1927) shows Custer and Crazy Horse fighting.

KATE BIGHEAD

During Custer's Last Stand, some soldiers saw that they were about to be killed. Before that could happen, they took their own lives. Kate Bighead was a Cheyenne woman whose nephew died in the battle. She said, "I saw a soldier shoot himself by holding his revolver at his head. . . . Right away, all of them began shooting themselves or shooting each other."

The desperate battle later called Custer's Last Stand ended in less than an hour. Surviving soldiers among Custer's group scattered into the nearby gullies and steep ravines. None made it out alive. Only Custer's trumpeter, Martini, lived. Delivering Custer's message to Benteen saved Martini's life.

Gunsmoke lingered in the air. Dead and wounded soldiers and Indians lay on the hillside. After Custer died, Benteen's and Reno's forces fought on for another thirty-six hours without water. Sitting Bull finally stopped the fighting. He told the warriors to let some white soldiers live so they could tell others about the Indians' power and might.

scalp: to cut the skin and hair from someone's head

Both U.S. soldiers and Indians had been known to scalp enemies. They also disfigured, or damaged, dead bodies. Native Americans believed the souls of disfigured dead were doomed to wander the earth forever. After this battle, warriors stripped blue uniforms off dead soldiers and damaged their bodies. Strangely, Custer's body was stripped but not disfigured. He had not worn his military uniform and had a shorter haircut for battle. Warriors may not have recognized him.

A total of 268 U.S. soldiers died at the Battle of Little Bighorn. Among the dead were Tom and Boston Custer, Custer's nephew Harry Armstrong Reed, and his brother-in-law Lieutenant James Calhoun. At home, Custer's wife, Libby, and other women waited. They sang hymns and prayed.

CHARLES CORN

Native American men fought fiercely to protect their women and children. Charles Corn was a Lakota warrior at the Battle of Little Bighorn. He later explained, "The soldiers wanted to kill us so we had to fight for our lives. [Soldiers] tried to get our children and wives, so I was willing to die fighting for them that day."

About forty Indians died in the battle, along with some of Custer's Indian scouts. Native American women who had lost loved ones wailed. They mourned by gashing their legs with pieces of flint, cutting their hair ragged, and smearing their bodies with ash. Soldier William O. Taylor said of the Indian dead, "In many [an Indian home] lay a cold red form brought from the nearby field of battle, the lifeless form of a husband and father."

After the battle, the Native Americans left the valley and retreated into the mountains. They had won a great victory.

NEXT QUESTION

WHY DID SITTING BULL FEEL TROUBLED AFTER THE BATTLE?

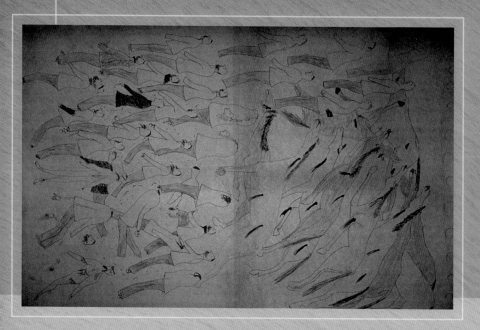

SIX DEFEAT FROM VICTORY

Spirits had warned Sitting Bull in his Sun Dance vision. The spirits told him that his people should not disfigure and steal from white people's bodies. Yet they had. He felt that a curse would fall upon his people as punishment.

On June 27, 1876, U.S. soldiers under Terry and Gibbon came upon the Little Bighorn battlefield. They found the bodies of more than two hundred soldiers and seventy horses. For two days, decaying corpses had lain in the blazing summer heat. A horrible smell filled the air. Soldiers quickly threw dirt and sagebrush over the corpses of their friends and fellow fighters. Someone snipped a lock of Custer's hair for his widow, Libby. Then the soldiers buried Custer alongside his brother Tom.

For the Native Americans who survived the battle, bitter hardship followed. Eager to seek revenge, the army pursued the Sioux and the Cheyenne. The army attacked villages, burned tipis, and killed the Indians' horses. This left Native Americans with no way to hunt. They had little food or warm clothing for the harsh winter ahead. One by one, chiefs and their bands of Indians surrendered. But Crazy Horse and Sitting Bull refused.

After the Battle of Little Bighorn, U.S. Cavalry officers told Sitting Bull *(left)* that he and his people must return to their reservation. Sitting Bull refused. Western artist Frederick Remington captured the scene in this 1876 painting.

By December 1876, Crazy Horse and two thousand Lakota Sioux and Cheyenne were wandering in the Wyoming and Montana territories. Freezing temperatures caused many illnesses and deaths. Crazy Horse's wife fell ill with a lung disease called tuberculosis. Their baby girl had died earlier of cholera. Crazy Horse felt he had to give up to save his starving people. On September 6, 1877, he and three hundred families surrendered at Fort Robinson in Nebraska.

At the fort, U.S. agents led Crazy Horse to a cramped, foul-smelling prison cell. He realized he was under arrest. He pulled out a knife and struggled to break free. One of his former warriors and friends, Little Big Man, had become a police officer for the U.S. government. He tried to calm Crazy Horse.

Bad Heart Bull showed Crazy Horse struggling with U.S. officers in this image, created in about 1900. As a historian, Bad Heart Bull often made handwritten notes on his drawings.

> "That night . . . there was more and more mourning . . . until it was all over the camp. [Crazy Horse] was brave and good and wise. He never wanted anything but to save his people."
> —Black Elk, Oglala warrior, recalling the 1877 death of Crazy Horse

CRAZY HORSE MEMORIAL
The Crazy Horse Memorial is a huge statue being carved into the Black Hills of South Dakota. It is 17 miles (27 km) southwest of Mount Rushmore.

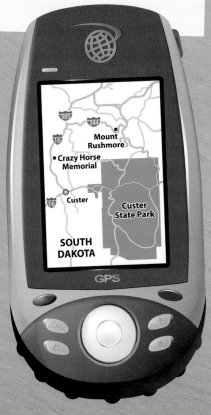

But Crazy Horse pulled away and the guards stabbed him. Bleeding, he fell to the ground. He died a few hours later. The next day, his parents took his body away. No one knows where on the South Dakota prairie Crazy Horse is buried.

The army chased Sitting Bull and the Hunkpapa north. In May 1877, the group crossed into Canada, where the U.S. Army could not follow. In Canada, Sitting Bull's people struggled to find food. Fewer and fewer buffalo roamed the open plains. In poor health and broken in spirit, Sitting Bull returned to the United States. On July 20, 1881, he surrendered at Fort Buford in Montana Territory.

At the fort, Sitting Bull's eight-year-old son, Crow Foot, handed his father's gun to the officer in charge of the fort. "I wish it to be remembered," Sitting Bull said, "that I was the last man of my tribe to surrender my rifle."

Sitting Bull hoped to join his people at Standing Rock Reservation. But instead, soldiers locked him in Fort Randall's prison for two years. After prison he was sent to the reservation. In 1885 the U.S. government allowed Sitting Bull to leave the reservation. He experienced things far different from his life on the Great Plains. For the first time, he rode on trains, visited museums, and met important white officials. Later that year,

Sitting Bull joined Buffalo Bill's Wild West Show. The show was led by Buffalo Bill Cody, a white soldier, scout, and hunter. Members of Cody's show toured the country demonstrating their Wild West skills—shooting guns, riding horses, and roping cattle.

Sitting Bull *(left)* poses with Buffalo Bill Cody *(right)* during Sitting Bull's 1885 tour with Buffalo Bill's Wild West Show. As part of the show's cast, Sitting Bull signed autographs, posed for photos, and reenacted famous western battles.

After four months, Sitting Bull went home to Standing Rock Reservation. He returned to life with his wives and children in a sod-roofed, dirt-floored log cabin on Grand River, close to his birthplace.

In early December 1890, Sitting Bull had a disturbing vision. A bird warned him that his own people, the Lakota, would kill him. Soon after, Indian police and U.S. cavalry soldiers arrived at the reservation. The police were worried that Sitting Bull might join the growing Ghost Dance movement.

On December 15, 1890, police officers dragged Sitting Bull out of his cabin. An angry crowd of Sitting Bull's friends and Ghost Dancers shouted at the officers. Shots rang out. When the smoke cleared, twelve Native Americans lay dead. Among them were Sitting Bull and his seventeen-year-old son, Crow Foot.

WHAT WAS THE GHOST DANCE?

In the late 1880s, many Lakota living on reservations became part of the Ghost Dance movement. The Ghost Dance was a ceremony to help heal the body and spirit. During the ceremony, ghost dancers often fell into a kind of dream called a trance. They called upon the spirits of their ancestors to help drive white people away. Sometimes they sang these words: "My Father, have pity on me! I have nothing to eat, I am dying of thirst—everything is gone!"

U.S. officials thought the Ghost Dance was more than a religious ceremony. They believed it was part of a dangerous movement that led some Lakota to rebel against white laws and rules. In 1890 the U.S. government called in troops to try to stop the Ghost Dance movement.

WOUNDED KNEE

On December 28, 1890, cavalry soldiers surrounded a Native American camp near Wounded Knee Creek in South Dakota. The camp was filled with members of a Lakota band called the Miniconjou. The U.S. Army was worried that the Ghost Dance movement was growing. They feared that Lakota warriors would rise up against the army.

On December 29, the soldiers told the Miniconjou to surrender their weapons. A few young warriors protested. Suddenly shots rang out. In response, soldiers began shooting everywhere. They killed more than two hundred men, women, and children. Twenty-five soldiers were also shot. The remaining Indians fled to the hills. In time, they turned over their weapons and surrendered. The Wounded Knee Massacre ended the Ghost Dance movement.

Soldiers buried Sitting Bull's body at Fort Yates in North Dakota. "We laid the noble old Chief away without a hymn or a prayer or a sprinkle of earth," said soldier John F. Waggoner. Many consider Sitting Bull one of the greatest chiefs that ever lived on the Northern Plains.

At the same time, newspaper stories about the Battle of Little Bighorn praised Custer as a hero.

The Custer National Cemetery was built in 1879 on the Little Bighorn battlefield to honor the soldiers and scouts who died there. Burials of U.S. soldiers in the cemetery continued until 1978.

Libby Custer added to her husband's legend by writing three best-selling books about him. Modern historians agree that Custer was a skilled fighter. But he is no longer considered a hero.

Monuments to Sitting Bull and Crazy Horse stand in modern-day South Dakota and the Black Hills. The Little Bighorn Battlefield National Monument in Montana honors both Native Americans and 7th Cavalry soldiers.

The Battle of Little Bighorn was the last large conflict between whites and Native Americans to take place in the nineteenth century. Three strong leaders—George Armstrong Custer, Sitting Bull, and Crazy Horse—all played a part on that historic day.

THE BATTLEFIELD
The U.S. Park Service has run the Little Bighorn Battlefield National Monument since 1940. The park is 65 miles (105 km) southeast of Billings, Montana.

NEXT QUESTION

HOW DO WE KNOW ABOUT THIS BATTLE?

Primary Source: Survivors' Stories

The best way to learn about any historical event is with primary sources. Primary sources are created near the time being studied. They include diaries or journals, letters, newspaper articles, documents, speeches, pamphlets, photos, paintings, and other items. They are made by people who have firsthand knowledge of the event. Much of what we know about the Battle of Little Bighorn comes from those who survived—Native Americans and U.S. soldiers.

After the battle, Sitting Bull recalled, "There were a great many brave men in that fight. They [the soldiers] were shot down like pigs. One by one the officers fell. The Long Hair stood like a sheaf of corn with all the ears fallen around him. He killed a man when he fell. He laughed . . . he laughed [and] he fired his last shot. He rose up on his hands and tried another shot, but his pistol would not go off."

Seventeen-year-old cavalry soldier William O. Taylor survived the battle. He described it as a "death-encircled ride in the valley and up the bluffs, pursued by a howling mass of red warriors." The warriors, Taylor wrote, cared "nothing for their own lives, were determined to save their families, or die."

He recalled waiting with Reno's men at the top of the hill that night. "In the darkness a deep feeling of sadness came over our hearts," Taylor wrote. "Scattered around us nearby were the fresh, and shallow graves of some who had fallen in our midst that afternoon. . . . No ceremony, a little trench right where they fell, a few inches of earth thrown over them, to be washed off by the first rain."

TELL YOUR LITTLE BIGHORN STORY

Imagine you are a survivor of the 1876 Battle of Little Bighorn. Weeks after the battle, you are interviewed by a newspaper writer. You tell the writer your story of the conflict.

WHO are you? A U.S. soldier? A Native American warrior? A Native American woman or child?

WHAT is your name?

WHERE are you from?

WHAT happened to you on the day of the battle?

WHY do you think the battle was necessary? Or how do you think it could have been avoided? How has your life changed because of the battle?

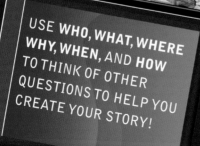

USE **WHO, WHAT, WHERE WHY, WHEN,** AND **HOW** TO THINK OF OTHER QUESTIONS TO HELP YOU CREATE YOUR STORY!

Timeline

ca.1831

Sitting Bull is born near Grand River in modern-day South Dakota.

1839

George Armstrong Custer is born in New Rumley, Ohio.

1841

Crazy Horse is born in the Black Hills of South Dakota.

1860s

The U.S. government begins creating reservations—lands where they claim Native Americans can live and hunt free from white settlers.

1864

U.S. soldiers kill more than 150 Cheyenne at **Sand Creek**, Colorado.

1866–1868

Battles break out between Native Americans and U.S. soldiers along the Bozeman Trail in Montana and Wyoming. The battles are called Red Cloud's War.

1868

Some Native American leaders and U.S. government representatives sign the Fort Laramie Treaty, creating the Great Sioux Reservation. In November, Custer attacks a Cheyenne village at the Washita River in Oklahoma.

1869

The transcontinental railroad is finished. It links the eastern and western coasts of the United States.

1874

Custer leads an expedition to the Black Hills and discovers gold.

1876

The U.S. government orders Native Americans to settle on reservations by January 31. In early June, Sitting Bull leads a Sun Dance ceremony at Rosebud Creek in Montana. On June 17, Crazy Horse attacks General Crook's soldiers at the Battle of Rosebud Creek. The Lakota and other Native American groups move to an encampment on the Little Bighorn River. On June 25, Native American forces defeat the U.S. Army in the **Battle of Little Bighorn.**

1877

Crazy Horse surrenders to U.S. officials. He is killed while resisting arrest.

1879

The U.S. government builds Custer National Cemetary on the Little Bighorn battlefield.

1881

Sitting Bull surrenders.

1885

Sitting Bull travels with Buffalo Bill's Wild West Show.

1890

Sioux Indian police kill Sitting Bull. Cavalry soldiers kill a peaceful group of Miniconjou Lakota people at Wounded Knee Creek in South Dakota.

1940

The U.S. Park Service begins running the Little Bighorn Battlefield National Monument.

1991

U.S. president George H. W. Bush signs a law creating an Indian Memorial at the Little Bighorn Battlefield National Monument. The memorial honors the Native Americans who died during the battle.

Source Notes

4 *Bismarck (South Dakota) Tribune*, June 17, 1874, quoted in James Welch and Paul Stekler, *Last Stand at Little Bighorn*, DVD (Boston: WGBH, 2005).

8 Mark Hollabaugh. "Ethnoastronomy of the Lakota," quoted in Dee Brown, *Bury My Heart at Wounded Knee* (New York: Henry Holt & Co., 1970), 273.

14 Welch and Stekler, *Last Stand at Little Bighorn*.

4 James Welch and Paul Stekler, *Killing Custer* (New York: W. W. Norton, 1994), 82.

17 Evan S. Connell. *Son of the Morning Star: Custer and Little Bighorn* (San Francisco: North Point Press, 1984), 115–116.

15 George A. Custer. *My Life on the Plains: Or, Personal Experiences with Indians* (1874; repr., Norman: University of Oklahoma Press, 1962), 19–21.

18 Hollabaugh, 449.

24 Welch and Stekler, *Killing Custer*, 152.

24 Peter Panzeri, *Little Big Horn 1876: Custer's Last Stand* (Oxford, UK: Osprey Publishing, 1995), 41.

25 Bill Yenne, *Sitting Bull* (Yardley, PA: Westholme, 2008), 94.

28 W. A. Graham, *The Custer Myth: A Source Book of Custeriana* (1953; repr., Lincoln: University of Nebraska Press, 1981), 71.

29 Yenne, 96.

30 Stephen Ambrose, *Crazy Horse and Custer* (New York: Anchor Books, 1996), 435.

31 Graham, 297.

32 Welch and Stekler, *Killing Custer*, 171.

33 William O. Taylor, *With Custer on the Little Bighorn* (New York: Viking Penguin, 1996), 176.

33 Graham, 57.

38 Taylor, 176.

40 Yenne, 284.

37 John G. Neihardt, *Black Elk Speaks* (Lincoln: University of Nebraska Press, 1961), 147.

39 Colin F. Taylor, *The Plains Indians* (London: Salamander Books, 1994), 245.

42 Yenne, 100.

42 Taylor, 45.

42 Ibid., 51.

Selected Bibliography

Connell, Evan S. *Son of the Morning Star: Custer and Little Bighorn*. San Francisco: North Point Press, 1984.

Crummett, Michael. *Tatanka-Iyotanka: A Biography of Sitting Bull*. Tucson, AZ: Western National Parks Association, 2002.

Custer, Elizabeth Bacon. *Boots and Saddles*. New York: Harper & Brothers, 1885.

Custer, George A. *My Life on the Plains: Or, Personal Experiences with Indians*. 1874. Reprint, Norman: University of Oklahoma Press, 1962.

Gardner, Mark L. *George Armstrong Custer*. Tucson, AZ: Western National Parks Association, 2005.

Graham, W. A. *The Custer Myth: A Source Book of Custeriana*. 1953. Reprint, Lincoln: University of Nebraska Press, 1981.

PBS. *New Perspectives on the West*. 2001. http://www.pbs.org/weta/thewest/program (September 17, 2010).

Sill, Joe, Jr. "The Battle of the Little Bighorn." *Custer Battlefield*. 2009. http://www.custerbattlefield.org/battle.shtml (September 17, 2010).

Taylor, Colin F. *The Plains Indians*. London: Salamander Books, 1994.

Further Reading and Websites

Cunningham, Chet. *Chief Crazy Horse*. Minneapolis: Twenty-First Century Books, 2000. Read the inspiring story of the great Native American leader and warrior.

Dolan, Edward F. *The American Indian Wars*. Minneapolis: Twenty-First Century Books, 2003. Throughout the 1800s, conflicts among white settlers and Native Americans on the Great Plains grew worse. Dolan details how the major battles shaped the fate of Native Americans, the West, and the nation.

Levine, Michelle. *The Sioux*. Minneapolis: Lerner Publications Company, 2007. Learn about the languages, history, and culture of Lakota, Dakota, and Nakota people and their modern communities.

Little Bighorn Battlefield
http://www.nps.gov/libi/index.ht
This National Park Service website has information on the battle, photos of the area and the battlefield monument, a map, and more.

Roop, Peter, and Connie Roop. *Sitting Bull*. New York: Scholastic, 2002. The Roops draw upon period images and letters and speeches from Sitting Bull and from his friends and family to create this biography.

Theunissen, Steve. *The Battle of the Little Bighorn*. Broomhall, PA: Mason Crest Publishers, 2002. Theunissen describes the events leading up to the conflict and the details of the battle.

Walker, Paul Robert. *Remember Little Bighorn: Indians, Soldiers, and Scouts Tell Their Stories*. Des Moines: National Geographic Children's Books, 2006. Using primary source material, Walker tells the story of the fateful battle.

Index

Photo Acknowledgments

The images in this book are used with the permission of: © iStockphoto.com/DNY59, p. 1; © Jakub Pavlinec/Dreamstime.com, pp. 1 (background) and all horse fur backgrounds; © iStockphoto.com/sx70, pp. 3 (top), 7, 16 (bottom), 17 (top), 19 (right), 20 (bottom), 23 (top), 25 (top), 32, 33 (top), 39, 40 (top); © iStockphoto.com/Ayse Nazli Deliormanli, pp. 3 (bottom), 43 (bottom left); © iStockphoto.com/Serdar Yagci, pp. 4, 43 (background); © Bill Hauser & Laura Westlund/Independent Picture Service, pp. 4-5 (top); © Stapleton Collection/CORBIS, pp. 4-5 (bottom); © iStockphoto.com/Andrey Pustovoy, pp. 5, 40 (bottom); © Jill Battaglia/Dreamstime.com, p. 5 (inset); © North Wind Picture Archives, p. 6; © CORBIS, p. 8; © SuperStock/SuperStock, p. 9; © Bridgeman Art Library/SuperStock, p. 10; Courtesy, History Colorado (Lindneux Collection, Scan # 20020087), pp. 11 (top), 44; The Art Archive/W. Langdon Kihn/NGS Image Collection, p. 12; © Laura Westlund/Independent Picture Service, pp. 13, 29, 37 (inset), 41 (inset); The Denver Public Library, Western History Collection, X-33801, p. 14; © Apic/Hulton Archive/Getty Images, p. 15; National Archives, p. 16 (top, 77-HQ-264-854); The Denver Public Library, Western History Collection, Miss Louise Stegner, X-31243, p. 18; © Everett Collection/SuperStock, p. 19 (left); Library of Congress, pp. 20 (top, LC-USZ62-54652), 24 (LC-DIG-cwpbh-00101), 38 (LC-USZ62-21207); The Denver Public Library, Western History Collection, David Frances Barry, B-142, p. 21 (top); © Chuck Haney/Danita Delimont/Alamy, p. 22; The Denver Public Library, Western History Collection, David Frances Barry, B-924, p. 23 (bottom); The Denver Public Library, Western History Collection, David Frances Barry, B-547, p. 25 (bottom); The Granger Collection, New York, pp. 26, 27 (top), 34, 43 (bottom right); © Stapleton Collection/Heritage/The Image Works, pp. 28, 30; © World History/Topham/The Image Works, p. 31; © MPI/Archive Photos/Getty Images, p. 35; © Stapleton Collection/HIP/The Image Works, p. 36; © iStockphoto.com/Talshiar, pp. 37, 41 (top); © Michael Lewis/National Geographic/Getty Images, p. 40 (inset); © Amos Bad Heart Buffalo/The Bridgeman Art Library/Getty Images, p. 45.

Front cover: © MPI/Archive Photos/Getty Images. Back cover: © Jakub Pavlinec/Dreamstime.com.